I0844974

Say hello to your new best friends!
This Cute Animals themed nursery art is a set of 12 high-quality 8x10" prints of original illustrations plus 12 high-quality 5x7" prints.

The Sweet Bunny, the Smiley Giraffe, the Lovable Lion, the Cute Elephant, and their friends are little critters eager to be displayed.

INSTRUCTIONS
· Cut out and frame the pages for an outstanding wall decoration.
· The page size is 8.5x11" providing you an extra white border and guide lines for easy cutting and framing.
· Perfect for 8x10" and 5x7" frames.
· Frames are not included.

INTERESTING
· Perfect for any room of the house!
· Reproductions of original watercolor illustrations.
· High-quality art print.
· Exceptional contrast and color saturation.
· Feeding not necessary!

Step 1:
Cut the illustrations out of the book.

Step 2:
Frame the illustrations.

Step 3:
Hang them on the wall and enjoy!

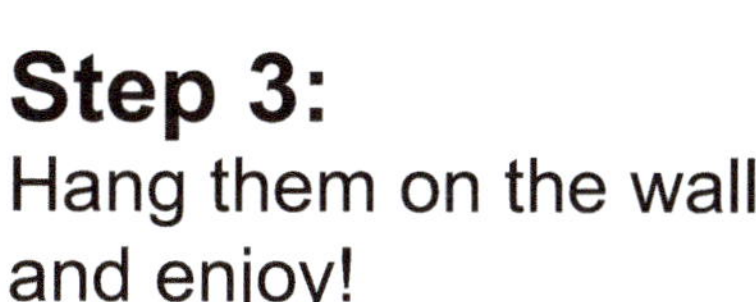

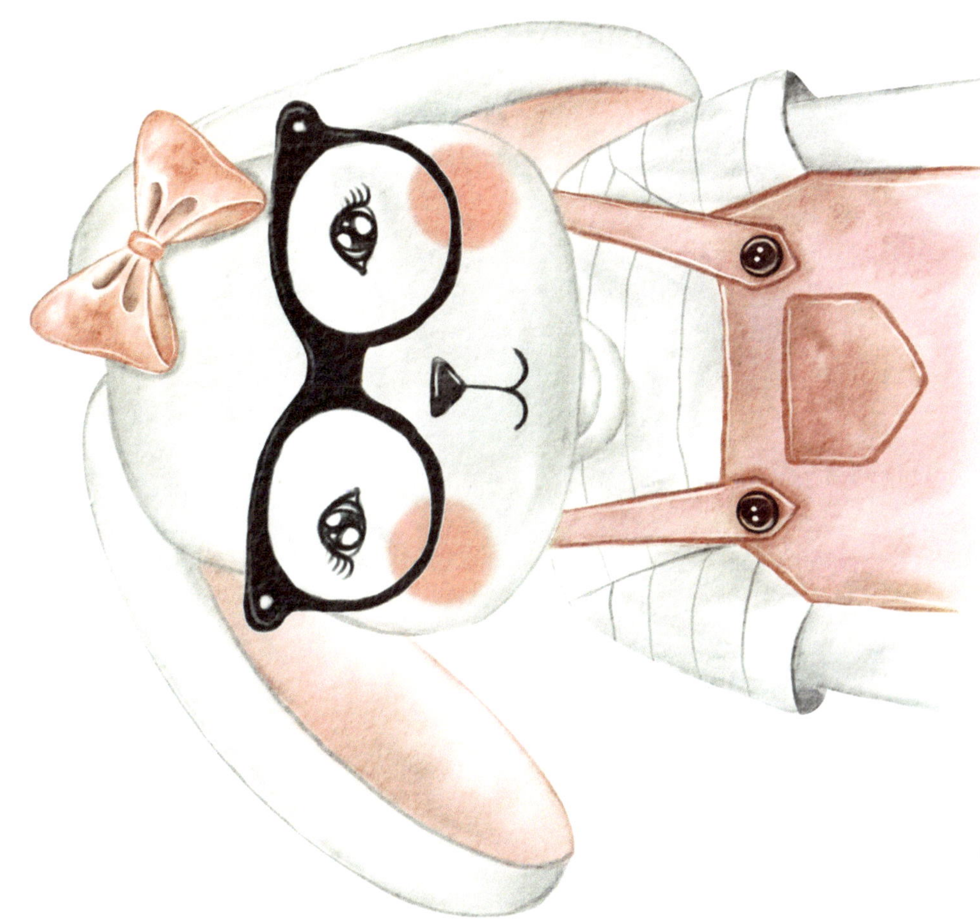

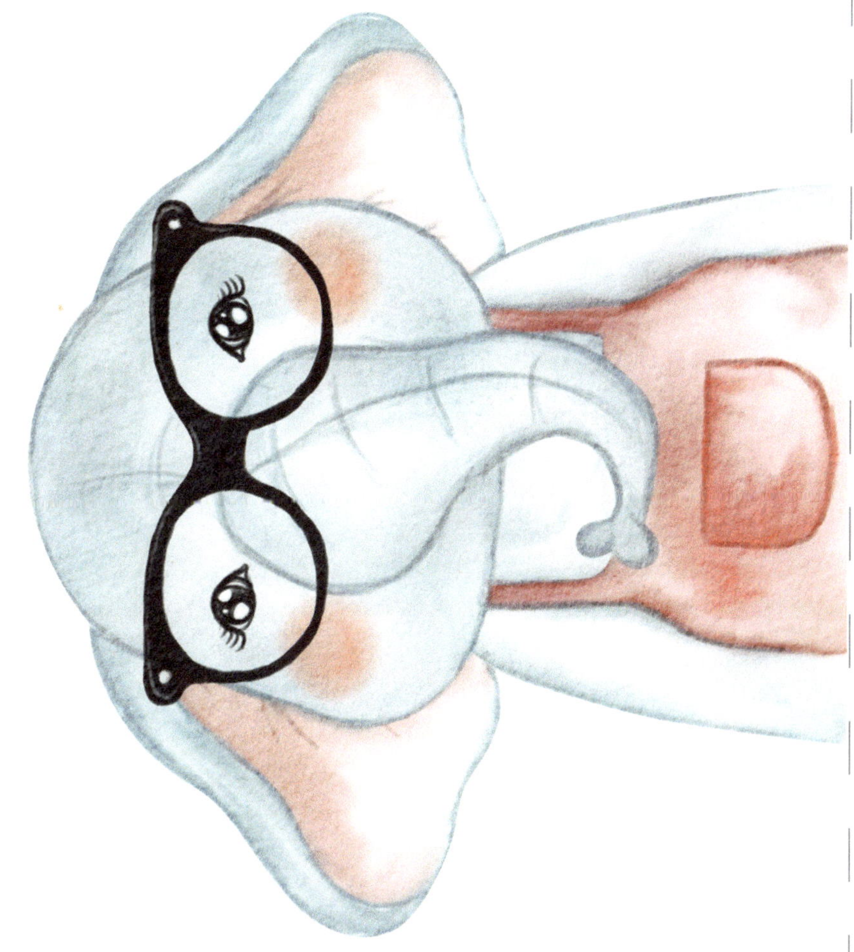

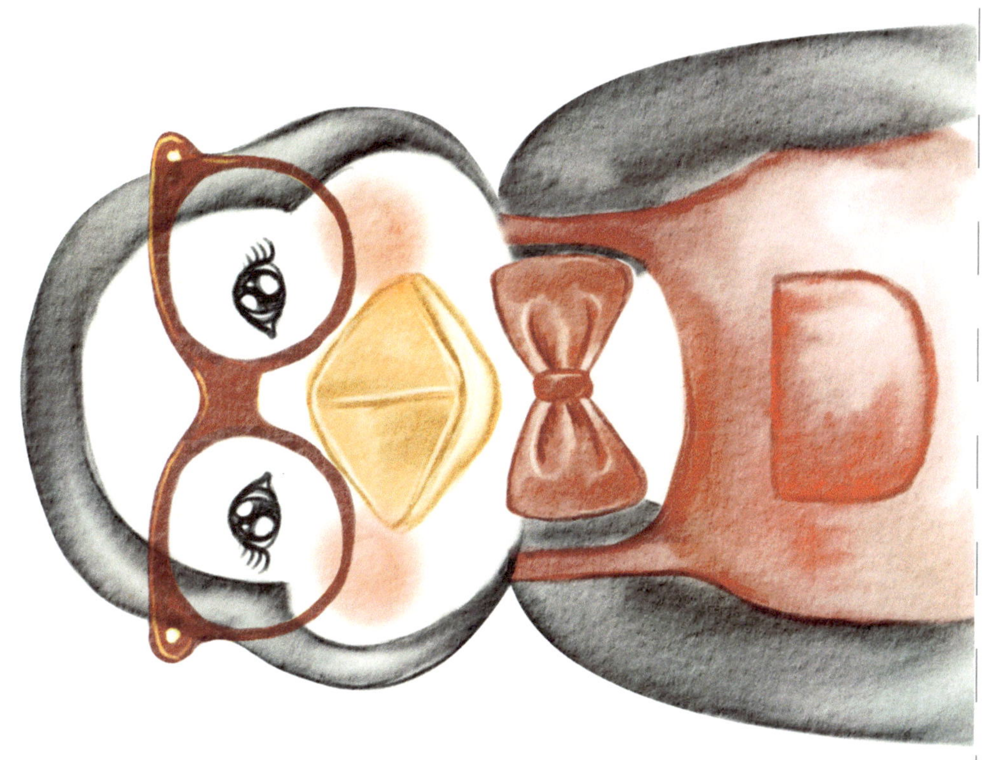

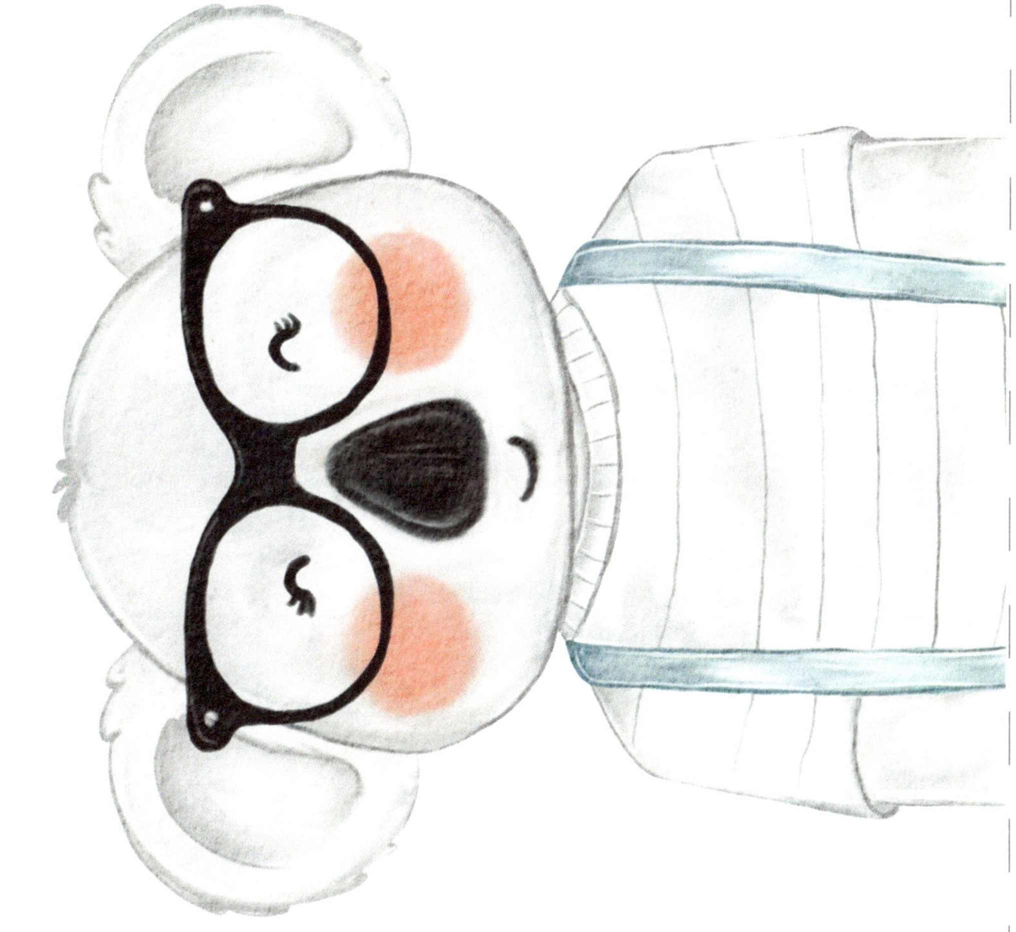

www.creatystyle.com
Visit our website for more products
or customizations !